THIS BOOK BELONG TO

Happy Valentine's Day

Happy
Valentines
Day

HAPPY
VALENTINE'S DAY

BE
MINE

BE MY
VALENTINE

I LOVE U

BE MY VALENTINE

Happy Valentine's Day!

BE
MINE
VALENTINE
MAIL BOX

www.ingramcontent.com/pod-product-compliance
Lightning Source LLC
Chambersburg PA
CBHW080241260726
48658CB00008B/3193